Sericulture:

The Proper Employment of Women in 19th Century China

By

Grace E. Wright

Cover Photographs by Wesley Wright

(2005)

TABLE OF CONTENTS

SERICULTURE *1*

Chart A *45*

Chart B *47*

ENDNOTES *49*

REFERENCES *55*

INDEX *65*

SERICULTURE

The Greeks knew China as *Serica*, the land of silk.[1] Silk products were one of China's first exports and perhaps one of its oldest industries. The earliest attested date for domestication of the silkworm in China was by 7500 BC.[2] Silk weaving in China can be traced back at least to the *Shang* period (c154-1045 BC) and Chinese silk seems to have reached northern India by the fourth or third centuries BC.[3] This was a time in India's history that ushered in the beginning of interest in Chinese products, including silk. But silk was special. Unlike other manufactured commodities silk was predominately produced by women. In fact, the production of silk was the only officially recognized employment for women. From the time of the *Chou Dynasty* (c1122 – 221 BC) sericulture, the work of cultivating silkworms and weaving was written about as the special profession of woman.[4] This employment, from the skill and energy of woman, contributed wealth directly to both the family and the empire. According to *Confucius* women contributed their portion of the tax burden by making silk just as men contributed grain.[5] So, for women, silk production had government sanction. During the nineteenth century this role afforded women an opportunity to push the boundaries of the female role as it had existed in traditional Chinese society.

Since the *Northern Chou Dynasty* (AD 557-581) the officially accepted legend about the origin of sericulture reinforced the acceptance of women's employment in the silk industry. The legend began with the Emperor *Chin Nong* who first cultivated the

2

mulberry tree in 2800 BC. But it was his successor *Huan-ti*, the legendary patron of agriculture, in 2602 BC, who recognized the value of sericulture as a means to contribute to the wealth of his nation and to the happiness of his people. So, with this in mind, he encouraged his young wife *Si-Ling Chi* to investigate silkworm rearing. The Chinese empress, per her husband's wishes, attentively devoted herself to the endeavor. After observing the silkworm spinning fiber on the leaves of a white mulberry tree *Si-Ling Chi* had a large quantity of silkworms collected. She took a personal interest in raising them, reeling the silk thread and weaving it into cloth. Once she mastered the technique she demonstrated it to the court ladies.[6] From this legendry imperial beginning the silk industry of China was born. It began with a woman and would continue to be the industry of woman.

The silk industry was one of traditional China's most important industries, both in terms of the state's interest and the peasant's livelihood. With this interest in mind the state throughout the history of China encouraged women to participate fully in sericulture. Yearly the Empress offered sacrifices to insure successful rearing of the silkworm.[7] The <u>Book of Songs</u>, from the *Chou Dynasty*, stipulated that a woman's public office was her weaving and spinning – to stop engaging in silk's manufacture, was not proper. In the <u>Biographies of Eminent Women</u>, written *by Lieh Nü Chuan* during the *Later Han Dynasty* (AD 25-220), several women were profiled to illustrate how a woman's keen concern in spinning and weaving won them the highest praise and contributed economically at home. Additionally, "this theme of women's responsibility for spinning and weaving continued in the *Tang* period (AD 705-907); a book called <u>Notes on</u>

Women (*Nulunyu*) recommended spinning and weaving as special skills for women."[8]

During the *Ming* and *Ch'ing* Dynasties (1436-1911) provincial governments used memorials to consistently encourage women to engage in the textile handicraft industry.[9] The *Ch'ing* introduced sericulture into new provinces with tax incentives and distribution of free mulberry saplings. Officials felt that suffering peasants could bring additional income into the household from woman's weaving.[10] Thus, the skills of spinning and weaving were significant in the ideal of Chinese womanhood. From the gentry on down, the ideal wife was responsible for rearing silkworms and clothing her husband in silk.[11] This model still existed in 1842 when Robert Montgomery Martin wrote that "the Empress breeds silkworms, and weaves herself, to encourage this branch of industry."[12]

W. H. Medhurst, in 1838, reports "the Chinese are confessedly a well-clothed nation, and except where poverty prevents, the people are seen attired in silks and crepes, as commonly as we [Europeans], appear in cloth and leather."[13] This is certainly an overstatement but silk was popular within Chinese society; in fact, fifty-five percent of all raw silk produced in China was for the domestic market. (For an understanding of the sumptory laws in China see *Tung-Tsu Chu*, Law and Society in Traditional China.)

Originally, silk production appears to have been for the manufacture of clothing but quickly a variety of other items were produced. Silk in different forms was given as personal gifts between individuals, used as religious offerings at temples and shrines, made into decorations for lances and buildings, used for barter and sold for cash. In addition it was used to fulfill tax obligations to the government as tax "in kind" payments. Thus as late as 1884 some portions of *Shansi* province were singled out to continue to pay silk "in kind" and individuals were allowed to commute it to money payment.[14] The government had many uses for the store of silk: one traditionally had been as an item of exchange to be given to barbarians as a peace keeping device. This exchange was one of the beginnings of external trade and introduced silk outside of China. As silk became known, it also became a commodity demanded by non-producing countries.

Silk production, largely a peasant household activity, was quite decentralized and unregulated by the government. Peasant households were free to produce any quantity. In an effort to produce as much as possible, peasant women "spun and wove when they had finished a day's heavy work in the fields, or during their spare time between household tasks."[15] Traveling through *Szechwan* in 1871 Baron Richthofen notes that:

Of manufactures no one occupies so many hands as those connected with the working of silk into various fabrics. There are large portions of Ching-tu-fu, where in every house spinning, dyeing, weaving, and embroidering are the occupations of the inhabitants. In the country, the reeling, washing, bleeching [sic] of the raw material are even in winter a conspicuous business.[16]

Another foreigner traveling through South China noted that: "One can travel for a day on a passage boat through the region and see nothing but mulberry fields as far as the eye can reach."[17] These observations show the immense commitment of land and labor that certain parts of China had to sericulture. Silk would be produced in all but two provinces, but by late *Ch'ing* times, sericulture flourished particularly in four areas of China:

(1) Chekiang and Kiangsu in the lower Yangtze – Lake T'ai region, with main centers in and around Hangchow, Hu-chou, Soochow, and Nanking; (2) Kwangtung, with centers at Shun-te and Canton; (3) Szechwan, with main centers at Chengtu, Chia-ting, and Chungking; (4) Shuantung [sic][18]

Silk was produced in stages, each requiring constant "hands on" care, 90% of which was done by women.[19] In 1847 an observer notes and reports in the Chinese Repository that "females devote much of their time and their talents to this occupation, they are either engaged in feeding and rearing the worms, winding off the cocoons, or in general tendency of the magnanerie [silkworm nursery]."[20] As well, Margaret E. Burton in 1918 observed that, "All forms of sericulture, (too), are carried on by Chinese women, raising the silkworm, spinning the raw silk into thread, and weaving the thread into the finished silk."[21]

This production traditionally complemented agriculture, as it was a seasonal occupation that could be done between crops. It also contributed financially to the household – a need that the government recognized. In 1844, *Wan Chu*, the Treasurer of *Kiángsí* encouraged the feminine occupation of tending silkworms as a means to help the peasant obtain money to pay the household's tax burden.[22]

Silk is the product of the silkworm, the larva of the moth *bombyx mori*. When hatched, the larva consumes large quantities of leaves. Although silkworms will eat the leaves of various types of trees, only if they are fed the leaves of the mulberry tree will they produce silk of high quality. Mulberry trees are hardy and can be grown in almost any type of soil and climate as long as there is adequate water, drainage and fertilizer. Mulberry trees were planted between agricultural crops, on hills, along the banks of canals or wherever there was space. The object of mulberry cultivation was to obtain large quantities of good-quality leaves having a high nutritive value. In April 1886 the explorer B. C. Henry witnessed thousands of boys, women and girls stripping the first of the year's crop of mulberry leaves and packing them in baskets. This process was done every six weeks with an utmost yield of six crops in a year.[23] From an economic point of view, the large eating capacity of the silkworm was an important consideration. Growing mulberry leaves became, in itself, a profitable undertaking.[24] Peasant households specializing in this commodity could turn a profit. Markets sprang up to accommodate the need and brokers arose to handle various transactions. They accepted advance orders for leaves and they advanced short-term loans to the small peasant engaged in sericulture.[25] So, providing leaves became a specialized business to supplement a household's income.

Silkworms, the consumer of mulberry leaves, were cared for largely by the labor of women.[26] There were three crops a year, each requiring feeding every two hours for about five weeks at a stretch. During this time all other activities in the peasant household and in the village were suspended. "People shut their doors and did not visit each other. The local *yamen* did not collect taxes or hold judicial proceedings. And all local schools closed so that the children could help out."[27] One estimate is that a crop of 700,000 worms weighs about one pound at birth but after eating steadily and shedding their skins four times, known in Chinese as the four "sleeps," they will weigh at maturity nearly five tons. By this time they will have actually eaten twelve tons of mulberry leaves and will produce between 116 and 175 pounds of raw silk.[28]

With proper care and nourishment the silkworms grow rapidly and at the end of 17 to 40 days they stop eating and emit a long whitish liquid thread that solidifies in air and builds the silk cocoon in one to two days. If left alone, in from eight to twelve days, the moth will break the cocoon to escape. This rebirth was damaging to the cocoon breaking the silken thread.[29] Therefore, several means to prevent this damage were developed. The most common in rural areas was to heat the cocoons over charcoal to kill the pupae inside. Once this was accomplished the cocoon was ready to be unwound.

The thread from each cocoon could extend to 1,700 meters[30] and throughout spring and summer foreign travelers witnessed hundreds of women sitting by their doors unwinding the gossamer threads from the cocoons. This process, silk reeling, was done by putting the cocoons in warm water and stirring and rolling them about gently with the hands to rise up the ends of the filaments that were caught with the left hand. The cocoons were moved through the water several times to unravel them leaving the pure fine silk lying beneath. Holding the fine silk in one hand, with a perforated ladle in the other, the cocoons were kept in the water while winding the silk on a wheel. Reeling commenced by first taking up the threads in the left hand, in order to keep them from tangling and then turning the reel with a foot-board. The thread had to be kept smooth and even with the hand and fingers at all times.[31] When the reeling was done the raw silk thread was ready for sale or weaving.

During much of the nineteenth century raw silk and woven silk were produced in one of two ways. Raw silk was produced by either "self-employed" peasants or by the "putting out" system. The "putting out" system was orchestrated by entrepreneurs who owned warehouses and employed agents who either distributed cocoons for reeling or raw silk and looms for weaving to the peasant households. Within a specified time limit the agents collected the finished products. Wages were paid by the piece usually coupled with some kind of allowance or stipend.[32] The entrepreneurs provided the financing and assumed the entire risk for the fluctuation in the market.[33] The peasant households contributed time and risked no financial set-back, they were paid a set fee for their work established at the time of the contract.

"Self-employed" peasants were able to carry out the production process with more independence but they also assumed more risk. They often carried out multiple stages in silk production and marketed the finished raw silk products to silk merchants. Women were allowed to take the silk to markets and deal with the male silk merchants.[34] Since, during the nineteenth Century, the silk market was highly stable in terms of price and demand, the self-employed sericulturalist could make a tidy profit with little investment. But they suffered a loss if climate or internal political problems affected either the mulberry leaf market or the cocoon market.

Beginning in the 1860's the "putting-out" system gained favor. Thus, there was a sub-division of the labor process between mulberry cultivation, silkworm rearing and processing silk. Groups of peasantry devoted themselves exclusively to different stages of the process using the traditional labor intensive practices that had been handed down in the family. Only occasionally did a peasant household engage in silk production from start to finish. Consequently, the peasantry in the silk industry lost the control they formerly possessed over their raw materials and labor product.

The mulberry peasant, living on a narrow margin, had to sell the leaves to the market as soon as they were ready to prevent spoilage and in order to pay

16

rent and loans[35] while at the same time the silkworm cultivator had to buy within specific time parameters no matter what the cost. Cocoons and raw silk were supplied by firms to peasants at the company's discretion. Peasants lost control over quantity and personal time management in order to meet factory requirements and deadlines.

The peasant involved in the "putting-out" system had little contact with silk markets. It was the company agent or the broker who came to villages in April, May and June from trading firms. These individuals served as middlemen and collectors of output.[36] It was, then, the broker who sold the finished products through the commission houses directly or indirectly through the local wholesale merchants.[37] The merchants in turn sold to *hongs* either for domestic or foreign consumption.

The silk demand increased as urban and export markets expanded and provided added opportunities to supplement a household's income. Silk contributed 30 to 40% of the value of all exports until just before the 1911 Revolution.[38] More households devoted resources to producing silk intermediary products to top this income source. Women, especially the widows of peasants, turned to full-time spinning and weaving in order to support their families.[39] Their personal labor was able to provide a new source of revenue. They no longer were dependent on the generosity of relatives now they were dependent on an industry.

By the late 1850's silk production provided part-time or full-time employment for several million farm families. In some cases, peasants were able to use the supplemental income to move up the social and economic ladders. Such a case was the merchant-farmer *Bi Fenglian* of *Zechuan* County, *Shandong*. *Bi* owned less than 30 *mu* of land when he began his silk-weaving activities. With the money from his family's silk labor he expanded his enterprise to over 300 *mu* of land and more than 20 looms, all operated by hired workers. Upon his death in 1840 his grandson, *Bi Yuanrong* continued to expand the family business with a hat-making shop. The *Bi* family now owned over 600 *mu* of land and employed about 200 workers.[40] This was rare, but none the less clear indication that there was money to be made in the silk industry.

As early as the 1070's or 1080's[41] silk workers formed associations or guilds to represent their labor and trade to protect their interests. Peter J. Golas defines a guild as

> ...an urban fraternal association whose members usually engaged in a single economic activity; often, but not necessarily, shared a common geographical origin that was not the city in which the guild was located; and joined together under the protection of one or more patron deities to promote their common economic and other interests.[42]

These guilds were not supported or restrained by the government in any way; rather, they acted as independent agents. Guilds acted as government tax collectors in exchange for monopolistic rights.[43] As such the guild was able to exercise almost complete control over their respective trades and membership. Membership was mandatory for all workers in the craft and all were compelled to obey the guild's rules and pay dues.[44] As a monopoly the guilds fixed prices, established the quantity and quality of silk produced,[45] and supplied the standard weighing scales on which all transactions were based.[46] They also sponsored apprentices recruited from kinsmen, provided for the needs of indigent members and bereaved dependents, and settled problems among the membership. Guilds did not necessarily act in unison with each other; instead each set their own rules. The *Soochow* silk guild, as an example, saw to it that *Soochow* silk was measured by the *Soochow* "foot" and no other measurement[47] even though this was not consistent with other guilds. The guilds also organized and supplied workers for factories.

The silk factory in the nineteenth century was not a new idea. Factories had been run by the Chinese government ever since the *Han* Dynasty. These factories were part of the Imperial Factory system, which was set up and financed by the state. The Imperial Silk Factories supplied the Imperial household with luxury silk products and silk for state conducted foreign trade. "By the early *Ch'ing* Dynasty (1644-1911), only the [Imperial] factories at *Hangchow, Soochow* and *Nanking* were still of importance for the court, while those of outlying districts and provinces had been largely abandoned."[48] These were not modern factories in the Western sense – they relied on the traditional labor intensive hand process for silk production. They bought raw silk from local peasants linking local production to government procurement.

In the early *Ch'ing* Dynasty, Imperial Silk Factories employed as many as two thousand looms and seven thousand artisans and laborers of various other types. As hired workers, they were paid wages either by the piece or on a daily or monthly rate and often supplemented with food allotments, paid in kind.[49] A vast majority of the labor was done by female reelers and weavers who worked and lived in the government run workshops under rather unpleasant working conditions.[50] When Sarah Conger saw the Imperial Silk Factories in 1909 she was both appalled and amazed to see that such small, dirty places could turn out such a beautiful product. Silk made in Imperial factories was not for sale; therefore, it did not meet the export demand.[51]

Exports of raw silk had risen from 10,000 *piculs* (1 *picul* = 110 pounds) in 1840 to 102,000 *piculs* in 1890 and accounted for 32.6% of China's exports in 1867.[52] By 1880 household production of raw silk could not meet the demand or quality needed for foreign export so the industry moved toward factory production using Western technology. Silk manufactured in steam-powered filatures was superior to hand-reeled silk in regularity, winding, cleanliness and elasticity; and was more suitable for use on power looms overseas.[53]

Before 1895 at least six steam silk reeling facilities were established in China.[54] The first, the *Ewo* Filature, was established at *Shanghai* in 1862 by the British import-export firm of Jardine Matheson & Co. From inception the *Ewo* Filature faced opposition from the local silk merchant guild and had difficulty securing a reliable supply of high quality cocoons. These factories along with a sustained cumulative loss forced it to close in 1869. In 1878 the *Kee Chong* Silk Filature Company, founded by the American import-export firm of Russell and Co., opened in *Shanghai* and was followed, in 1881, by the British filature Iverson and Company (*Kung-ho yung*). That year also saw the first Chinese owned filature at *Shanghai*, *Chang Kee*. This filature was founded by *Huang Zuoqing*, a Chinese silk merchant.[55] The *Ewo* Filature was reestablished in 1881 followed by several other filatures such as the *Ruilun* Filature in 1894. The *Ruilun* Filature was one of the largest and best equipped in *Shanghai*. It was a partnership between a local well known silk merchant and *Wu Shaoqing*, the comprador of Arnhold Karberg & Company. By 1898 there were reportedly 27 filatures centered in *Shanghai* with about 4,000 reels and roughly 20,000 laborers[56] -- most of whom were young women and children recruited from the surrounding countryside and housed in company built dormitories.[57]

The Cantonese silk-reeling industry began in 1872 when a Cantonese merchant, *Ch'en Ch'i-yan,* founded the *Jichanglong* Filature, the first Chinese-owned modern factory in China in *Nanhai* County. *Ch'en Ch'i-yan* made his wealth as an overseas merchant and was now ready to enlarge his economic base. He opened the filature outside of *Canton* to be close to cocoon production and the local skilled female work force. By 1881 at least ten other filatures were in operation in *Nanhai* County employing women between the ages of 13 and 24.[58] By 1900 over 100 filatures were located in the *Canton* Delta with the largest being completely mechanized filatures. They operated with an estimated average work force of about five hundred women employed for cocoon peeling and sorting, silk reeling, finishing, re-reeling and waste preparing. It is interesting to note that supervisors and workers in steam engine rooms were usually men.[59] These filatures supplied 85% of *Canton's* raw silk for export in 1900.[60]

Initially, most filatures were built and managed by individual proprietorships and partnerships founded by groups of British, American, French and Chinese investors. Such enterprises required relatively little initial capital investment to construct and operate. Sericulture technology was relatively simple compared to other industries such as mining but the return could be great. What they needed was cheap skilled labor and to convince people of the value of the industry.

All the filatures established during the nineteenth century experienced considerable difficulties initially. There was opposition to the noise of the machinery, the presence and height of smoke stacks that damaged local geomantic configuration and injury to workers who were unfamiliar with machinery. Concern also came from the government in the 1880's. In *Kiangsu* and *Chekiang*, where 50% of the households in rural areas were engaged in some stage of silk production, the local official (*Taotai*) feared that filatures would "deprive Chinese who depend on silk reeling of their means of support," and this would "lead to trouble and complication."[61]

Editorials and advertisements were placed in local newspapers expounding the value of filatures. They rebutted the idea that filatures were reducing profits for local raw silk producers. They declared that, in fact, the need for more cocoons helped hinterland sericulture producers. This they said gave the peasant added opportunities and supported the *Confucian* policy of "emphasizing the peasants and suppressing the merchants."[62] There really was no competition in as much as the home industry supported internal Chinese use and the factories pushed goods to the export ports.

In 1822, *Soochow* Prefecture, documents were issued by local authorities in an effort to clarify and to diffuse problems between the silk establishments and the weavers. In the documents authorities emphasized the need for non-rural weavers to live on contracted wages alone. Workers were forbidden to sell raw materials or woven products for personal benefit. Workers could not organize collective actions for higher wages, strikes or volunteering as arbitrators in labor disputes. Weavers not in good standing with an employer were barred from employment within the silk industry.[63] This clearly favored the manufactories and undermined city workers, making conditions conducive for unrest.

As a result of increasing numbers of urban silk workers, the rural sericulturalists were restless, as cocoons and hand-reeled silk were diverted for the use of export-oriented filatures. These materials became scarce and expensive for the rural silk weavers. Bad crop years during the nineteenth century exasperated the situation and reduced income of the traditional rural producers. The attitudes for both the rural and urban worker in the silk industry was to become apparent through social unrest focused against the newly formed filatures.

Silk workers in Canton organized an armed strike in 1850 and another in 1851. They protested price speculation. They not only broke into and damaged a filature, they also attacked the residences of those who continued to make silk in their households.[64] These actions produced delays in the delivery of foreign export contracts. In 1881 a similar incident occurred when the silk weaver's guild gathered for their annual feast in *Nanhai* County. The weavers recently had suffered from growing scarcity and rising prices of hand reeled silk as the new steam filatures diverted cocoons for their production. The farmers had also suffered from a poor harvest of cocoons that year. These grievances along with gambling and drinking incited the crowd of one thousand. They marched to *Yuhouchange* Filature and smashed machinery and looted taking more than 10,000 *piculs* of cocoons along with other items. Local villagers defended the filature against the farmers, capturing two of the rioters and killing two others. The following day several thousand rural weavers returned to the village to free their colleagues. The villagers met this attempt with gun fire. The local militia were sent in and reestablished peace. For some time after, the government posted troops in the village to maintain the shaky calm.

The calm was broken in 1888 when confrontation between several hundred weavers and filature workers again erupted into armed combat. This ended with six or seven people killed and many wounded. *Ch'en's* filature survived but a smaller silk-reeling machine was invented to appease the protesters.[65]

B. C. Henry reported in 1886 that; "An attempt was made a few years ago to introduce machinery into one of the great silk establishments near *Sai-tsin*, but the place was twice mobbed within a short time and the owners compelled to remove the machinery."[66] But by the turn of the century it was clear that factory production of silk, requiring fewer workers, for export had won. Filature silk exports had displaced hand-reeled silk in *Canton* by 1890 when it cornered three quarters of the export market at *Canton*. At *Shanghai* it was not until 1911 that filature silk overtook hand-reeled silk.[67] Filatures capable of year-round operation placed new demands on the traditional pattern of the supply of cocoons and changed the nature of sericulture. Factories exercised control over labor, monitored time and instituted rules and regulations into family and social life.

Silk weaving, on the other hand, did not go through the same transition to modernization as silk reeling. The first modern silk weaving factory in China appeared with the establishment of the *Yi Chang* Silk Factory of *Hangchow* in 1905.[68] And as late as 1933 H. D. Fong wrote that, "In China silk weaving is carried on exclusively by handlooms and silk handloom weaving constitutes one of the leading rural industries."[69]

Men involved in silk manufacture used traditional social patterns to gain access and to stabilize their position in the silk industry. They used worker organizations, like guilds, to organize a power base as a group. They were not employed in areas that traditionally had been considered women's work; reeling, weaving, etc. Thus, there was not a competition for jobs between men and women. Men clashed against the formation of the industry itself through strikes and protest movements. Women, on the other hand, were not part of the Silkweaver's guilds nor were they involved in the strikes, but women did resist. Their resistance, however, was against social norms. They used their positions in the silk industry to acquire an independent and valued economic base to practice life styles different from the traditional role of wife.

Confucian morality required that women serve in the home and not mix in society.[70] But the silk industry had a different requirement. Society had already accepted and established through myth and custom the rightful employment of women in silk manufacture within the household. So when *Zhang Zhidong*, the *Huguang* Governor-General, set up silk-reeling filatures, it was not unorthodox to invite and appoint women laborers from *Shanghai* to train others. *Zhang* who had already established cotton mills in the north believed that hiring female workers violated Confucian morality. At least he felt this way for cotton but not for silk. When he established his silk filature, *Zhang* felt it was in fact "difficult to replace women with men, for silk-reeling was considered women's work alone."[71]

For peasant women spinning and weaving were significant abilities not as mere accomplishments but for vital economic reasons. Women who could spin and weave were great assets to peasant households, making them desirable wives.[72] Women had little to no legitimate authority or independent economic means in Chinese society, so marriage was the means used to secure a position and financial security in Chinese society. Even though a nineteenth century writer says "from the moment when she is joined in wedlock, she ceases to exist,"[73] marriage was the primary life option open to women.

Kay Ann Johnson characterizes Chinese society as having a "patriarchal-patrilineal-patrilocal configuration."[74] This configuration made women marginal members of the family system with little status or power in society. In response "women worked much of their lives to carve out some space in which their behavior and own sense of identity would not be totally dictated by dominant ideals of passive submission to male authority."[75] In their traditional role as a wife they gained some status and respect through bearing children – especially a son. Upon the son's marriage they gained authority as a mother-in-law and somewhat ended the isolation of marriage. As a foreign missionary traveling in the nineteenth century observed, women "never go anywhere to speak of, and live . . . . the existence of a frog in a well."[76]

During early industrialization female laborers came together as a group[77] to perform the tasks required to process goods for export, including silk. Women drawn into the work force[78] as female spinners and weavers moved to the cities for jobs in the new filatures.[79] They united to form groups or sisterhoods to provide social units to protect their interests. Work in the silk industry provided an end to isolation, some economic independence and a respectable, government sanctioned, position in society.

Two important alternatives to traditional marriage were developed in the Canton Delta. The first, "compensation marriage," worked through traditional marriage patterns to achieve loosening of the normal constraints on women in society. The second was, "women who dress their own hair" (*zishunü*), sisterhoods of women vowing to never marry. B. C. Henry attributed anti-matrimonial practices to the high-spirited disposition of women. He admired their spirit of independence and courage.[80] Both practices were to become linked to sericulture in several counties in *Guangdong* in the nineteenth century.

What in sericulture areas promoted anti-marriage practices? Anti-marriage practices began before modernization in the silk reeling industry.[81] It had grown in areas; where a high percentage of the population was involved in the silk industry;[82] where there was a mix between non-Han cultures and Han peoples; and where girls had value because of their contribution to the family wealth through labor in silk production. These areas also boosted low rates of female infanticide and footbinding of daughters was limited.[83] The families took pride in having their daughters work and accumulate wealth.[84] Women also acquired freedom of movement as they were allowed to travel to help neighbors reel silk for which they were paid a wage.[85] This income could be more than a man could make through agricultural endeavors and enhanced the woman's status in the family and raised her self-esteem.[86]

The Cantonese filature owners believed that single women made for a stable labor force because single women historically had better attendance records and they had fewer family obligations. They were the preferred work force.[87] Families, with some hesitation, also saw the benefit of having their daughters work in the filatures. Filatures provided comparatively high wages for a woman. This encouraged families, both natal and in-law, not to resist anti-marriage practices by daughters.

"Compensation marriage" brides made a contract with their husband's family to pay cash compensation to allow her independence from the role of wife.[88] She married and stayed at her husband's home for three days after which she returned to her natal family.[89] She often took extensive measures to protect her virginity in the three days. She wanted to avoid pregnancy, a condition that would insure dismissal from a filature job.[90] After the marriage ceremony she either returned to her natal home or to her room at or near the filatures. She was obligated financially to support her in-laws and her husband. She was also obligated to purchase a concubine for her husband and support any children from the union. It was expected she would return in old age, but often this did not happen.[91]

Early in the nineteenth century the government pressured women to discontinue "compensation marriage".[92] So women turned to a different, more radical anti-marriage practice. This was called "women who dress their own hair." In this practice women

> . . . took a vow before a deity, in front of witnesses, never to wed. The vow was preceded by a hairdressing ritual resembling the one traditionally performed before marriage to signal a girl's arrival at social maturity."[93]

The ceremony released the woman from her natal family and released her family's obligation to support her.[94] This "anti-marriage" practice was more popular then its predecessor, "compensation marriage" because it was simpler and economically more profitable for the woman. Her money was her own.[95] It, however, raised social problems. Without a family the women had no one to care for her in old age and nowhere to put her ancestral tablet. These problems were addressed by the women themselves, who joined together in sisterhoods.[96]

Sisterhoods were groups of five to forty women joined together to perform most of the functions of a nuclear family.[97] The women often bought a common residence, cared for each other in sickness and old age, assisted financially when needed, cared for adopted children and performed the proper ancestor worship.[98] These women, through sericulture, were able to establish an independent economic base for themselves and carve a space out in society that was socially acceptable.

In the ancient times the Confucian structure had classified male Chinese persons and industry into four groups. (1) There were officials, who held government jobs (2) farmers, who cultivated the land (3) artisans, who finished the goods and (4) merchants who exchanged wealth and sold goods.[99] This structure along with the paternalistic nature of Chinese society presented an uphill struggle for women. To achieve independence from it and the traditional female role as a wife required a basic redefinition of where women fit into the Confucian structure – not an easy task. Sericulture, as the only government recognized employment, provided an avenue to launch the battle. Silk production made women's labor a crucially important necessity to the household and the country. This necessity increased the status of women in society and offered women the opportunity to work outside of the home. The development of silk reeling filatures in the nineteenth century offered a means to acquire an independent economic base to help secure alternate life styles, like the anti-marriage movements in *Kwangtung* province. Though these movements were not complete breaks from tradition they did offer broader choices for women's lives. These choices continued to grow in the twentieth century. The Spanish proverb "Patience and Perseverance will convert the mulberry leaf into silk"[100] sums up Chinese women's struggle to attain social and economic freedom – it would be a long road but something beautiful was to be produced.

Chart A
STAGES IN SILK PRODUCTION

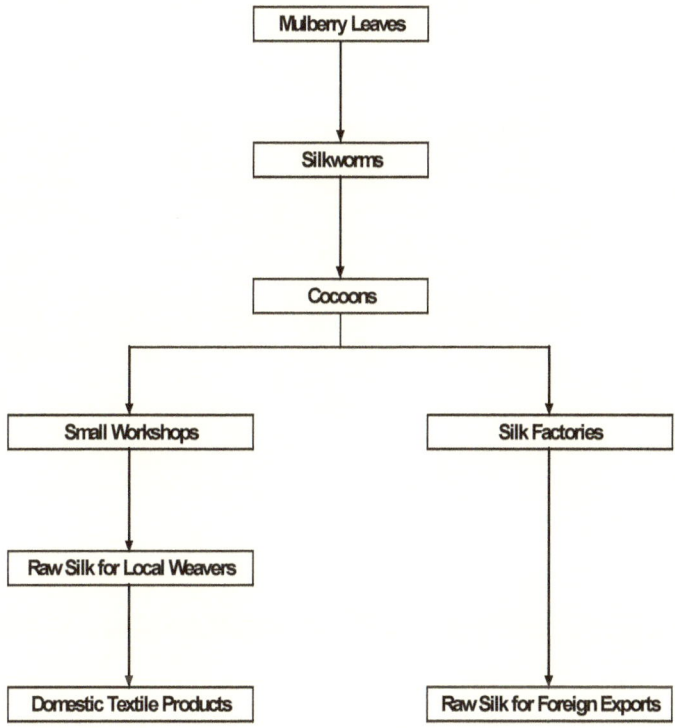

Adapted from Alvin Y. So. <u>The South China Silk District: Local Historical Transformation and World-System Theory</u>. Albany: State University of New York Press, 1986. p. 84.

Chart B

CHINA:1900

Provinces that had some sericulture in 1900

ENDNOTES

[1] Dr. Paul Michaud, lecture, Oakland University, 7 Sept. 1990.

[2] Jared Diamond, Guns, Germs, and Steel: The Fates of Human Societies. (New York: W. W. Norton & Company, 1999) 100.

[3] Jacques Gernet, A History of Chinese Civilization trans. J. R. Foster, (Cambridge: Cambridge University Press, 1972) 73.

[4] Chen Huan-Chang, The Economic Principles of Confucius and His School (New York: Longmans, Green & Co, 1911) 503.

[5] Chen 635.

[6] Thien-fu Li, "China's Silk Industry," Chinese Economic Journal 7 (1930): 134 and Clinton G. Gilroy, The History of Silk, Cotton, Linen, Wool, and Other Fibrous Substances: Including Observations on Spinning, Dyeing and Weaving (New York: C. M. Saxton, 1853) 9.

[7] Lucinda Pearl Boggs, Chinese Womanhood (Cincinnati: Jennings and Graham, 1913) 66.

[8] Bobby Siu, Women of China; Imperialism and Women's Resistance 1900-1949 (London: Zed Press, 1982) 82.

[9] Spinning and weaving was not limited to silk. In some areas, hemp and cotton were the chief fabrics. See Mark Elvin Patterns of the Chinese Past: A Social and Economic Interpretation. (Stanford University Press: 1973).

[10] Lillian M. Li, China's Silk Trade: Traditional Industry in the Modern World: 1842-1937 (Cambridge: Council on East Asian Studies, 1981) 135.

[11] Albert Richard O'Hara, The Position of Woman in Early China: According to the Lieh Nü Chuan "The Biographies of Eminent Chinese Women" (Westport: Hyperion Press, Inc., 1981) 35.

[12] Robert Montgomery Martin, China; Political, Commercial, and Social; In an Official Report to Her Majesty's Government (London: James Madden, 1852) 107.

[13] Walter Henry Medhurst, The Foreigner in Far Cathay (New York: Scribner, Armstrong and Company, 1873) 114.

[14] E-Tu Zen Sun, "Sericulture and Silk Textile Production in Ch'ing China," Economic Organization in Chinese Society ed. W. E. Willmott (Stanford: Stanford University Press, 1972) 80.
[15] Siu 82.
[16] Baron F. V. Richthofen, "Baron Richthofen's Letters: 1870-1872" (Shanghai: North-China Herald Office, 1872) 129. Baron Richthofen certainly overstated what he saw on his trip. Women who were needed for field labor (in poor households) were unlikely to have looms or time to weave.
[17] C. W. Howard, The Sericulture Industry of South China (Canton: Canton Christian College, 1923) 8.
[18] Sun 83.
[19] Lillian Li 148.
[20] Chinese Repository, XVIII (June 1849): 233.
[21] Margaret E. Burton, Women Workers of the Orient (West Medford: The Central Committee on the United Study of Foreign Missions, 1918) 24.
[22] Chinese Repository, XX (July, 1851): 306.
[23] B. C. Henry. Ling-Nam or Interior Views of Southern China; Including Explorations in the Hitherto Untraversed Island of Hainan (London: S. W. Partridge and Co., 1886) 66.
[24] Mark Elvin, "Skills and Resources in Late Traditional China," China's Modern Economy in Historical Perspective ed. Dwight H. Perkins (Stanford: Stanford University Press, 1975) 167.
[25] Sun 87.
[26] Susan Mann Jones, "The Ningpo Pang and Financial Power at Shanghai," The Chinese City Between Two Worlds ed. Mark Elvin and G. William Skinner (Stanford: Stanford University Press, 1974) 199.
[27] Lillian Li 19.
[28] John King Fairbanks, Trade and Diplomacy on the China Coast: The Opening of the Treaty Ports 1842-1854 (Cambridge: Harvard University Press, 1953) Vol. One: 290.
[29] D. K. Lieu, The Silk Industry of China (Shanghai: Kelly and Walsh, Limited, 1940) xi.
[30] Food and Agriculture Organization Services (FOA), China: Sericulture (Rome: Food and Agriculture Organization of the United Nations, 1980) 3.
[31] Alvin Yiu-cheong So, "Division of the Labor Process and Underdevelopment: A Study of the South China Silk Industry," The Insurgent Sociologist 11 (1982) 40-41.

[32] Lillan Li 51.

[33] Yoshinobu Shiba "Ningpo and Its Hinterland," The City in Late Imperial China ed. G. William Skinner (Stanford: Stanford University Press, 1977) 412.

[34] Shiba "Ningpo" 152.

[35] So "Division" 43.

[36] Betty Peh-T'I Wei, Shanghai: Crucible of Modern China (New York: Oxford University Press, 1987) 112.

[37] H. D. Fong Ph.D., Rural Industries in China (Tientsin: Chihli Press, Inc., 1933) 21.

[38] Robert Y. Eng, "Chinese Entrepreneurs, the Government, and the Foreign Sector: The Canton and Shanghai Silk-Reeling Enterprises, 1861-1932," Modern Asian Studies 18, 3 (1984): 354.

[39] Siu 38.

[40] Philip C. Huang, The Peasant Economy and Social Change in North China (Stanford: Stanford University Press, 1985) 96.

[41] Robert Y. Eng, Economic Imperialism in China: Silk Production and Exports. 1860-1932 (Berkeley: Institute of East Asian Studies University of California, 1986) 18.

[42] Peter J. Golas, "Early Ch'ing Guilds," The City in Late Imperial China ed. G. William Skinner (Stanford: Stanford University Press, 1977) 559.

[43] Eng, Economic 148.

[44] It is unclear if women were ever members of these guilds.

[45] Silk came in different grades, the finer grades were for government officials; these grades did not come off of peasant cottage looms but out of the silk factories in the cities. See Chart A

[46] Hosea Ballou Morse, The Gilds of China: With an Account of the Gild Merchant or Co-Hong of Canton 1909 (Taipei: Ch'eng-Wen Publishing Company, 1966) 31.

[47] Golas 572.

[48] Lillian Li 3.

[49] Sun 100.

[50] Joseph Needham and Dieter Kuhn, Science and Civilisation in China: Chemistry and Chemical Technology: Textile Technology: Spinning and Reeling (Cambridge: Cambridge University Press, 1988) Vol. 5 Part IX: 3.

[51] Sarah Pike Conger, Letters From China: With Particular Reference to the Empress Dowager and the Women of China (Chicago: A. C. McClurg & Co., 1909) 327.

[52] Huang 122.

[53] Eng, Economic 156.

[54] Ramon H. Myers, The Chinese Economy Past and Present (Belmont: Wadsworth, Inc., 1980) 130.

[55] Eng, "Chinese" 355.

[56] Ono Kazuko, The Chinese Women in a Century of Revolution: 1850-1950 1978. trans Kathryn Bernhardt, Timothy Brook, Joshua A. Fogel, Jonathan Lipman, Susan Mann and Laurel Rhodes. Ed. Joshua A. Fogel (Stanford: Stanford University Press, 1989) 24.

[57] The Earl of Ronaldshay, A Wandering Student in the Far East (Edinburgh: William Blackwood and Sons, 1908) Vol. 1: 52.

[58] Eng, "Chinese" 356.

[59] Eng, Economic 61.

[60] Eng, "Chinese" 106.

[61] Myers 127.

[62] Eng, "Chinese" 40.

[63] Sun 98.

[64] Chinese Repository, XX (July, 1851): 506-7.

[65] Eng Economic 151.

[66] Henry 67.

[67] Eng, "Chinese" 357.

[68] Lieu 162.

[69] Fong 21.

[70] Medhurst 114.

[71] Kazuko 24 (It is also the most physically unpleasant part of the process).

[72] Siu 82.

[73] Chinese Repositories II (Oct. 1833) 315.

[74] Kay Ann Johnson, Women, The Family and Peasant Revolution in China (Chicago: The University of Chicago Press, 1983) 9.

[75] Johnson 20.

[76] Johnson 14.

[77] Kazuko 23.

[78] Emily Honig, Sisters and Strangers: Women in the Shanghai Cotton Mills, 1919-1949 (Stanford: Stanford University Press, 1986) 11.

[79] Many women were sent either by their parents or in-laws on contract to the filatures. In this case at least part of the wages would have been sent back home.

[80] Henry 68.

[81] Patrice Andrea Sankar, The Evolution of the Sisterhood in Traditional Chinese Society: From Village Girls' Houses to Chai

T'angs in Hong Kong Diss Univ of Michigan, 1978 (Ann Arbor: UMI, 1978. 7813727) 33.

[82] Janice E. Stockard, Daughters of the Canton Delta: Marriage Patterns and Economic Strategies in South China, 1860-1930 (Stanford: Stanford University Press, 1989) 135.

[83] Stockard 175.

[84] Stockard 140.

[85] Stockard 151.

[86] Stockard 157.

[87] Eng, "Chinese" 360.

[88] Stockard 168.

[89] Marjorie Topley, "Marriage Resistance in Rural Kwangtung," Women in Chinese Society ed. Margery Wolf and Roxane Witke (Stanford: Stanford University Press, 1975) 247.

[90] Stockard 157.

[91] Topley 264.

[92] Sankar 33.

[93] Topley 247.

[94] Topley 261.

[95] Stockard 164.

[96] Stockard 169.

[97] There was a Buddhist base to the sisterhood groups . . . see Topley and Sankar to explore this topic.

[98] Sankar 8.

[99] Chen 367.

[100] Samuel Whitmarsh, Eight Years Experience and Oberservation in the Culture of the Mulberry Tree, and in the Care of the Silk Worm (Northampton: J. H. Butler, 1839) Title Page.

REFERENCES

Boggs, Lucinda Pearl. Chinese Womanhood.
        Cincinnati: Jennings and Graham, 1913.

Burton, Margaret E. Women Workers of the Orient.
        West Medford: The Central Committee on the
        United Study of Foreign Missions, 1918.

Chen Huan-Chang. The Economic Principles of
        Confucious and His School. New York:
        Longmans, Green & Co., 1911.

Chinese Repository. II (Oct. 1833): 313-316.

_____. XVI (May 1847): 223-236.

_____. XVIII (June 1849): 303-314.

_____. XX (July 1851): 506-507.

Conger, Sarah Pike. Letters From China: With Particular
        Reference to the Empress Dowager and the
        Women of China. Chicago: A. C. McClurg &
        Co., 1909.

Diamond, Jared. Guns, Germs, and Steel. New York:
        W.W. Norton & Company, 1999.

Elvin, Mark. The Pattern of the Chinese Past. Stanford: Stanford University Press, 1973.

_____. "Skills and Resources in Late Traditional China," in China's Modern Economy in Historical Perspective. Edited by Dwight H. Perkins. Stanford: Stanford University Press, 1975.

Eng, Robert Y. "Chinese Entrepreneurs, the Government, and the Foreign Sector: The Canton and Shanghai Silk-Reeling Enterprises, 1861-1932," Modern Asian Studies. 18, 3 (1984): 353-370.

_____. Economic Imperialism in China: Silk Production and Exports. 1861-1932. Berkeley: Institute of East Asian Studies University of California, 1986.

Fairbank, John King. Trade and Diplomacy on the China Coast: The Opening of the Treaty Ports 1842-1854. Cambridge: Harvard University Press, 1953. Vol. One.

Fong, H. D., Ph.D. Rural Industries in China. Tientsin: Chihli Press, Inc., 1933.

Food and Agriculture Organization Services. China: Sericulture. Rome: Food and Agriculture Organization of the United Nations, 1980.

Fortune, Robert. Three Years' Wanderings in the Northern Provinces of China. London: John Murray, 1847.

Gernet, Jacques. A History of Chinese Civilization. Trans. J. R. Foster. Cambridge : Cambridge University Press, 1989.

Gilroy, Clinton G. The History of Silk, Cotton, Linen, Wool, and Other Fibrous Substances : Including Observations on Spinning, Dyeing and Weaving. New York: C. M. Saxton, 1853.

Golas, Peter J. "Early Ch'ing Guilds," in The City in Late Imperial China. Edited by G. William Skinner. Stanford: Stanford University Press, 1977.

Henry, B. C. Ling-Nam or Interior Views of Southern China: Including Explorations in the Hitherto Untraversed Island of Hainan. London: S. W. Partridge and Co., 1886.

Honig, Emily. Sisters and Strangers: Women in the Shanghai Cotton Mills, 1919-1949. Stanford: Stanford University Press, 1986.

Howard, C. W. The Sericulture Industry of South China. Canton: Canton Christian College, 1923.

Howard, C. W. and K. P. Buswell. A Survey of the Silk Industry of South China. Hong Kong: Commercial Press, Ltd., 1925.

Hsiao, Kung-Chuan. Rural China: Imperial control in the Nineteenth Century. Seattle: University of Washington Press, 1967.

Huang, Philip C. The Peasant Economy and Social
      Change in North China. Stanford: Stanford
      University Press, 1985.

Johnson, Kay Ann. Women, The Family and Peasant
      Revolution in China. Chicago: The University
      of Chicago Press, 1983.

Jones, Susan Mann. "The Ningpo Pang and Financial
      Power at Shanghai," in The Chinese City
      Between Two Worlds. Edited by Mark Elvin
      and G. William Skinner. Stanford: Stanford
      University Press, 1974.

Kazuko, Ono. The Chinese Women in a Century of
      Revolution: 1850-1950. 1978. Trans. Kathryn
      Bernhardt, Timothy Brook, Joshua A. Fogel,
      Jonathan Lipman, Susan Mann and Laurel
      Rhodes. Ed. Joshua A. Fogel. Stanford:
      Stanford University Press, 1989.

Lang, Olga. Chinese Family and Society. New Haven:
      Yale University Press, 1946.

Lanning, G. and S. Couling. The History of Shanghai.
      Shanghai: Kelly & Walsh, Limited, 1921.
      Part I.

Lei, Y. W. and H. K. Lei. Report on a Steam Filature in
      Kwangtung. Canton: College Press, 1925.

Li, Lillian M. China's Silk Trade: Traditional Industry
      in the Modern World: 1842-1937. Cambridge:
      Council on East Asian Studies, 1981.

Li, Thien-fu. "China's Silk Industry," <u>Chinese Economic Journal</u>. 7 (1930) 1344-58.

Lieu, D. K. <u>The Silk Industry of China</u>. Shanghai: Kelly and Walsh, Limited, 1940.

Ma, Laurence J. C. <u>Commercial Development and Urban Change in Sung China (960-1279)</u>. Ann Arbor: Department of Geography University of Michigan, 1971.

Martin, Robert Montgomery. <u>China; Political, Commercial, and Social; In an Official Report to Her Majesty's Government</u>. London: James Madden, 1852.

Medhurst, Walter Henry. <u>China: Its State and Prospects</u>. London: John Snow, 1838.

_____. <u>The Foreigner in Far Cathay</u>. New York: Scribner, Armstrong and Company, 1873.

Michaud, Paul Ph.D. Lecture. Rochester : Oakland University, 7 Sept. 1990.

Morse, Hosae Ballou. <u>The Gilds of China: With an Account of the Gild Merchant or Co-Hong of Canton</u>. 1909. Taipei: Ch'eng-Wen Publishing Company, 1966.

_____. <u>The International Relations of the Chinese Empire: The Period of Conflict 1834-1860</u>. New York: Longmans, Green, and Company, 1910.

_____. The Trade and Administration of the Chinese
   Empire. 1907. Taipei: Ch'eng-Wen Publishing
   Company, 1966.

Myers, Ramon H. The Chinese Economy Past and
   Present. Belmont: Wadsworth, Inc., 1980.

Needham, Joseph and Dieter Kuhn. Science and
   Civilisation in China: Chemistry and Chemical
   Technology: Textile Technology: Spinning and
   Reeling. Cambridge: Cambridge University
   Press, 1988. Vol. 5 Part IX.

O'Hara, Albert Richard. The Position of Woman in
   Early China: Acording to the Lieh Nü Chuan
   "The Biographies of Eminent Chinese Women".
   1945. Westport: Hyperion Press, Inc., 1981.

Perkins, Dwight H. Agricultural Development in China:
   1368-1968. Chicago: Aldine Publishing
   Company, 1969.

Rawski, Evelyn Sakakida. Agricultural Change and the
   Peasant Economy of South China. Cambridge:
   Harvard University Press, 1972.

Richthofen, Ferdinand Paul Wilhelm. Baron
   Richthofen's Letters: 1870-1872. Shanghai:
   North China Herald Office, 1872.

Ronaldshay, The Earl of. A Wandering Student in the
   Far East. Edinburgh: William Blackwood and
   Sons, 1908. Vol. 1.

Sankar, Andrea Patrice. The Evolution of the
        Sisterhood in Traditional Chinese Society: From
        Village Girls' Houses to Chai T'angs in Hong
        Kong. Diss. U of Michigan, 1978. Ann Arbor:
        UMI, 1978. 7813727.

Shiba, Yoshinobu. Commerce and Society in Sung
        China. Trans. Mark Elvin. Ann Arbor:
        Michigan Abstracts of Chinese and Japanese
        Works on Chinese Works, 1970.

_____. "Ningpo and Its Hinterland," in The City in
        Late Imperial China. Edited by G. William
        Skinner. Stanford: Stanford University Press,
        1977.

Siu, Bobby. Women of China: Imperialism and
        Women's Resistance 1900-1949. London: Zed
        Press, 1982.

Smith, Arthur H. Village Life in China. 1899. Boston:
        Little, Brown & Co., 1970.

So, Alvin Yiu-cheong. "Division of the Labor Process
        and Underdevelopment: A Study of the South
        China Silk Industry," The Insurgent Sociologist.
        11 (1982): 39-47.

_____. The South China Silk District: Local
        Historical Transformation and World-System
        Theory. Albany: State University of New York
        Press, 1986.

Stockard, Janice E. Daughters of the Canton Delta: Marriage Patterns and Economic Strategies in South China, 1860-1930. Stanford: Stanford University Press, 1989.

Sun, E-Tu Zen. "Sericulture and Silk Textile Production in Ch'ing China," in Economic Organization in Chinese Society. Edited by W. E. Willmott. Stanford University Press, 1972.

Topley, Marjorie. "Marriage Resistance in Rural Kwangtung," in Women in Chinese Society. Edited my Margery Wolf and Roxane Witke. Stanford: Stanford University Press, 1975.

Wakeman, Frederic, Jr. Strangers at the Gate: Social Disorder in South China, 1839-1861. Berkeley: University of California Press, 1966.

Wei, Betty Peh-T'i. Shanghai: Crucible of Modern China. New York: Oxford University Press, 1987.

Whitmarsh, Samuel. Eight Years Experience and Observation in the Culture of the Mulberry Tree, and in the Care of the Silk Worm. Northampton: J. H. Butler, 1839.

INDEX

apprentices, *20*

Arnhold Karberg & Company, *24*

bombyx mori, *9*

Canton, *24, 28, 37*

Chang Kee Filature, *23*

Chekiang Province, *26*

Chin Nong, Emperor, *2*

Ch'ing Dynasty, *4, 5, 8, 21*

Chou Dynasty, *1, 2, 4*

compensation marriage, *35, 37, 38, 39*

Confucius, *2, 27, 40*

dormitories, *24*

Ewo Filature, *23*

export, silk, *17, 22, 25, 27, 28, 29, 30*

factory, silk, *16*

female infanticide, *36*

footbinding, *36*

foreign trade, *21*

guild, silk, *19, 20, 29, 32*

Han Dynasty, *4, 20*

Huan-ti, Emperor, *2*

Imperial Silk Factory, *20, 21, 22*

Iverson and Company, *23*

Jardine Matheson & Co., *23*

Jichanglong Filature, *24*

Kee Chong Silk Filature, *23*

Kiangsi Province, *9*

Kwangtung Province, *41*

loan, *11*

Ming Dynasty, *4*

Patron of agriculture, *2*

putting-out system, *15, 16*

riot, *29, 30*

Ruilun Filature, *23*

Russell and Co., *23*

self-employed, *15*

Shang Dynasty, *1*

Shansi Province, *6*

Si-Ling Chi, *3*

silk factory, *20*

silk reeling process, *13*

silkworm growing process, *12*

steam power, *22, 23, 25*

Szechwan Province, *7*

Tang Dynasty, *4*

tax, *6, 19*

Wan Chu, *9*

women who dress their own hair, *35, 38*

Yi Change Filature, *31*

Yuhouchange Filature, *29*